COCKTAILS

COCKTAILS

EDITED BY HELEN CHESTER

ST MARTIN'S PRESS · NEW YORK

ACKNOWLEDGEMENT

The publishers would like to thank The Zanzibar for their help in
contributing material to this book.
COCKTAILS

©Ward Lock Limited 1982
Illustrations © Orbis Verlag für Publizistik 1982

First Published in Great Britain
by Ward Lock Limited.

Cover photograph by Rob Matheson
Text filmset in Goudy Old Style
by Tradespools Limited, Frome, Somerset

Printed and bound in Spain.

ISBN 0-312-14634-5

Library of Congress Catalog Card Number: 82-62488

First U.S. Edition
10 9 8 7 6 5 4 3 2 1

CONTENTS

NOTE

It is important to follow *either* the metric *or* the imperial measures when using this book. Do *not* use a combination of measures.

All cocktails serve 1 person, unless indicated otherwise.

Basic Equipment and Ingredients

Equipment

COCKTAIL SHAKER – Two principal types are available: a standard shaker and a Boston shaker. The standard shaker has a base for ingredients, a built-in strainer and a fitted cap. It should never be filled more than four-fifths full. It is generally made of stainless steel. The Boston shaker, used professionally, is more complicated to handle.

MIXING GLASS – This is used for stirring cocktails. It should have a lip and be used in conjunction with a bar spoon.

HAWTHORN STRAINER – This is flat with a spring coiled round the edge. It is used mainly to strain stirred cocktails.

ICE BUCKET AND TONGS

ICE HAMMER

CORKSCREW AND BOTTLE OPENER

BITTERS BOTTLES WITH NOZZLES – These enable bitters to be obtained in 'dash' quantities.

TOTS, MEASURES, POURERS – These are very helpful in measuring correct quantities.

LIQUIDIZER OR BLENDER – Not vital but can be very useful.

SHARP KNIFE AND A CHOPPING BOARD – For slicing fruits and paring peel.

STRAWS

GLASSES – Stemmed, both small and medium in size

TUMBLERS AND LONG GLASSES

WINE GOBLETS

Note Do not over-fill glasses; allow for the inclusion of ice and decoration. Avoid using coloured glass as it will detract from its contents.

Ingredients

SPIRITS AND LIQUEURS – Gin, Scotch whisky, vodka, light and dark rum, brandy, Cointreau, tequila.

WINES AND FORTIFIED WINES – Port, sherry, red and white wine, dry, bianco and red vermouth, Campari.

MISCELLANEOUS – Grenadine, Angostura bitters, Tabasco sauce, Worcestershire sauce, oranges, lemons, limes, lime cordial, maraschino cherries, green olives and soda water.

ICE – This is best from a freezer rather than a domestic refrigerator.

To make cracked ice, use an ice hammer with a pointed head.

To crush ice, put ice blocks in a cloth, and hammer them hard with a mallet or rolling-pin.

To colour ice, add a few drops of edible food colouring before freezing.

SUGAR SYRUP – To make a readily available quantity, boil 450 g/1 lb sugar in 600 ml/1 pint water.

To make enough for individual recipes, boil 15 ml/1 tablespoon sugar in 30 ml/2 tablespoons water.

Brandy and Liqueur-based Cocktails

ABC

ABC

5 ICE CUBES
20 ML/¾ FL OZ ARMAGNAC
20 ML/¾ FL OZ BÉNÉDICTINE
1 DASH ANGOSTURA BITTERS
CHAMPAGNE
1 LEMON SLICE
2 ORANGE SEGMENTS
3 COCKTAIL CHERRIES

Crack two ice cubes and put in a shaker with
Armagnac, Bénédictine and bitters. Shake.
Crush remaining ice and put in a goblet. Strain
in contents of shaker and top up with
champagne. Decorate with lemon slice, orange
segments and cocktail cherries. Serve with a
straw.

ALEXANDER

2–3 ICE CUBES
20 ML/¾ FL OZ BRANDY
20 ML/¾ FL OZ CRÈME DE CACAO
20 ML/¾ FL OZ CREAM

Crack ice and put in a shaker with other ingredients. Shake well and strain into a cocktail glass.

APPLEJACK RABBIT

2–3 ICE CUBES
25 ML/1 FL OZ APPLEJACK or CALVADOS
20 ML/¾ FL OZ ORANGE JUICE
10 ML/2 TEASPOONS LEMON JUICE
5 ML/1 TEASPOON SUGAR SYRUP
1 DASH ORANGE BITTERS

Crack ice and put in a shaker with other ingredients. Shake well and strain into a cocktail glass.

APPLEJACK RABBIT

ANGEL'S KISS

40 ML/1½ FL OZ APRICOT BRANDY
15 ML/½ FL OZ CREAM
1 COCKTAIL CHERRY

Pour apricot brandy into a pousse-café glass. Add cream, pouring it gently over back of a spoon so that it floats on surface. Spear cherry on a cocktail stick and use to decorate.

BEL AMI

20 ML/¾ FL OZ BRANDY
20 ML/¾ FL OZ APRICOT BRANDY
20 ML/¾ FL OZ CREAM
30 ML/2 TABLESPOONS VANILLA ICE CREAM

Put all ingredients in an electric blender, mix, and serve in a wine goblet with ice cream wafers.

APRIL SHOWER

2 ICE CUBES
25 ML/1 FL OZ BRANDY
25 ML/1 FL OZ BÉNÉDICTINE
50 ML/2 FL OZ ORANGE JUICE
SODA WATER

Put ice in a tall goblet with brandy and Bénédictine. Stir well and add orange juice. Top up with soda water and serve with a straw.

BETWEEN THE SHEETS

2–3 ICE CUBES
20 ML/¾ FL OZ BRANDY
20 ML/¾ FL OZ WHITE RUM
20 ML/¾ FL OZ COINTREAU
15 ML/½ FL OZ ORANGE JUICE

Crack ice and put in a shaker with other ingredients. Shake well and strain into a large cocktail glass.

BRANDY COCKTAIL

1–2 ICE CUBES
40 ML/1½ FL OZ BRANDY
20 ML/¾ FL OZ RED VERMOUTH
2 DASHES ANGOSTURA BITTERS
PIECE OF LEMON PEEL (OPTIONAL)

Crack ice and put in a mixing glass. Add brandy, vermouth and bitters. Stir well and strain into a cocktail glass. Add piece of lemon peel, if liked.

BRANDY DAISY

2–3 ICE CUBES
25 ML/1 FL OZ BRANDY
15 ML/½ FL OZ LEMON JUICE
10 ML/2 TEASPOONS GRENADINE
SODA WATER
3–4 COCKTAIL CHERRIES

Crack ice and put in a shaker with brandy, lemon juice and grenadine. Shake well and strain into a champagne glass. Top up with soda water. Decorate with cherries and serve with a cocktail stick.

BRANDY CRUSTA

15 ML/½ FL OZ LEMON JUICE
15 ML/1 TABLESPOON CASTER SUGAR
2–3 ICE CUBES
50 ML/2 FL OZ BRANDY
5 ML/1 TEASPOON SUGAR SYRUP
3 DASHES MARASCHINO
2 DASHES ANGOSTURA BITTERS
SPIRAL OF LEMON PEEL

Dip rim of a large cocktail glass first in lemon juice, shaking off excess, then in sugar. Allow frosting to dry. Crack ice and put in a shaker with brandy, sugar syrup, maraschino and bitters. Shake well and strain into glass. Decorate with spiral of lemon peel.

BRANDY FIX

40 ML/1½ FL OZ BRANDY
20 ML/¾ FL OZ CHERRY BRANDY
15 ML/½ FL OZ LEMON JUICE
5 ML/1 TEASPOON SUGAR SYRUP
1 ICE CUBE
1 LEMON SLICE

Put brandy, cherry brandy, lemon juice and sugar syrup in a small goblet. Stir well. Crush ice and add to glass. Lay lemon slice on top. Serve with a straw.

BRANDY RICKEY

BRANDY HIGHBALL

3 ICE CUBES
25 ML/1 FL OZ BRANDY
5 ML/1 TEASPOON LEMON JUICE
5 ML/1 TEASPOON SUGAR SYRUP
1 DASH ORANGE BITTERS
SODA WATER

Crack one ice cube and put in shaker. Add
brandy, lemon juice, sugar syrup and bitters.
Shake well and strain into a tumbler. Add
remaining ice, and top up with soda water.

BRANDY RICKEY

3–4 LEMON SLICES
25 ML/1 FL OZ BRANDY
2–3 ICE CUBES
SODA WATER

Put lemon slices in a tumbler and press with a
spoon to make juice run. Add brandy and ice,
and top up with soda water. Serve with a straw
and spoon.

BRANDY SMASH

5 ML/1 TEASPOON CASTER SUGAR
5 ML/1 TEASPOON WATER
3 SPRIGS OF MINT
50 ML/2 FL OZ BRANDY
3–4 ICE CUBES
3–4 LEMON, LIME or ORANGE SLICES
2 STRAWBERRIES (OPTIONAL)
1–2 GRAPES (OPTIONAL)

Put sugar in a shaker with water. Add mint, crush well with a spoon and remove. Add brandy and shake well. Crush ice and put in a balloon glass. Strain contents of shaker into glass and decorate with lemon, lime or orange slices and other available fruits. Serve with a straw and spoon.

BUTTERFLY FLIP

2–3 ICE CUBES
1 EGG YOLK
15 ML/1 TABLESPOON CASTER SUGAR
25 ML/1 FL OZ BRANDY
25 ML/1 FL OZ CRÈME DE CACAO
25 ML/1 FL OZ CREAM
NUTMEG

Crack ice and put in a shaker with egg yolk, sugar, brandy, crème de cacao and cream. Shake very well and strain into a large cocktail glass. Grate a little nutmeg over top and serve with a straw.

BUTTERFLY FLIP

13

CALVADOS SMASH

2–3 ICE CUBES
30 ML/2 TABLESPOONS MIXED FRUIT
5 ML/1 TEASPOON CASTER SUGAR
SODA WATER
3 SPRIGS OF MINT
25 ML/1 FL OZ CALVADOS
3 DASHES CRÈME DE MENTHE
1 DASH BÉNÉDICTINE
APPLE JUICE
1 MINT LEAF

Crush ice, put in a tall glass and add fruit. Put sugar in a shaker and add a shot of soda water. Add sprigs of mint, and crush well with a spoon. Add Calvados, crème de menthe and Bénédictine, and shake well. Strain into glass and top up with apple juice. Decorate with mint leaf and serve with a straw.

CHARTREUSE TEMPTATION

25 ML/1 FL OZ GREEN CHARTREUSE
1 ICE CUBE
5 ML/1 TEASPOON LEMON JUICE
SPARKLING WINE

Pour Chartreuse into a tall champagne glass. Add ice and lemon juice, and top up with sparkling wine.

CHARTREUSE DAISY

2–3 ICE CUBES
40 ML/1½ FL OZ BRANDY
20 ML/¾ FL OZ GREEN CHARTREUSE
5 ML/1 TEASPOON LEMON JUICE
SODA WATER
3 COCKTAIL CHERRIES

Crack ice and put in a shaker with brandy, Chartreuse and lemon juice. Shake and strain into a shallow champagne glass. Top up with soda water and decorate with cherries. Serve with a cocktail stick.

CHICAGO COCKTAIL

2 ICE CUBES
40 ML/1½ FL OZ BRANDY
5 ML/1 TEASPOON COINTREAU
1 DASH ANGOSTURA BITTERS
SPARKLING WINE

Put ice in a mixing glass with brandy, Cointreau and bitters. Stir well and strain into a shallow champagne glass. Top up with sparkling wine and serve with a straw.

CHOCOLATE SOLDIER

2 ICE CUBES
25 ML/1 FL OZ BRANDY
20 ML/¾ FL OZ DRY VERMOUTH
10 ML/2 TEASPOONS CRÈME DE CACAO
1 DASH ORANGE BITTERS

Crack ice and put in an electric blender with other ingredients. Blend and pour into a shallow goblet.

COLORADO

2–3 ICE CUBES
20 ML/¾ FL OZ CHERRY BRANDY
20 ML/¾ FL OZ KIRSCH
20 ML/¾ FL OZ CREAM

Crack ice and put in a shaker with other ingredients. Shake well, strain into a cocktail glass and serve with a straw.

COFFEE COBBLER

3–4 ICE CUBES
25 ML/1 FL OZ BRANDY
STRONG COLD SWEETENED COFFEE

Crush ice and put in a goblet. Add brandy, and top up with coffee. Stir, and serve with a straw.

COPACABANA

2–3 ICE CUBES
15 ML/½ FL OZ BRANDY
25 ML/1 FL OZ APRICOT BRANDY
15 ML/½ FL OZ COINTREAU
15 ML/½ FL OZ LEMON JUICE
1 ORANGE SLICE

Crack ice and put in a shaker with brandy, apricot brandy, Cointreau and lemon juice. Shake well and strain into a large cocktail glass. Decorate with orange slice and serve with a straw.

DELICIOUS SOUR

DELICIOUS SOUR

2–3 ICE CUBES
1 EGG WHITE
5 ML/1 TEASPOON SUGAR SYRUP
15 ML/½ FL OZ LEMON JUICE
25 ML/1 FL OZ CALVADOS
25 ML/1 FL OZ APRICOT BRANDY
SODA WATER
2 APPLE SLICES

Crack ice and put in a shaker with egg white,
sugar syrup, lemon juice, Calvados and apricot
brandy. Shake very well and strain into a goblet.
Top up with soda water and fix apple slices on
rim of glass. Serve with a straw.

DIJON FIZZ

2–3 ICE CUBES
50 ML/2 FL OZ CRÈME DE CASSIS
40 ML/1½ FL OZ KIRSCH
SODA WATER
CLUSTER OF BLACKCURRANTS (OPTIONAL)

Crack ice and put in a shaker with crème de
cassis and kirsch. Shake well and strain into a
goblet. Top up with soda water and decorate
with a cluster of fresh blackcurrants,
if available.

GEORGIA MINT JULEP

10 ML/2 TEASPOONS CASTER SUGAR
65 ML/2½ FL OZ WATER
4 SPRIGS OF MINT
3 ICE CUBES
25 ML/1 FL OZ BRANDY
25 ML/1 FL OZ APRICOT BRANDY
4 APRICOT or PEACH SLICES
1 LEMON SLICE
1 LIME SLICE
1 COCKTAIL CHERRY

Put sugar and water in a mixing glass, add three sprigs of mint and crush gently with a teaspoon. Remove mint. Crush ice and put in a tumbler. Add mint-flavoured sugar syrup, brandy and apricot brandy. Decorate with apricot or peach slices, lemon and lime slices, cherry and remaining sprig of mint. Serve with a straw and a spoon.

GINGER DAISY

1 PIECE PRESERVED GINGER
2–3 ICE CUBES
15 ML/½ FL OZ BRANDY
15 ML/½ FL OZ LEMON JUICE
5 ML/1 TEASPOON ORANGE SYRUP
5 ML/1 TEASPOON SUGAR SYRUP
GINGER ALE

Dice ginger and put in a shaker with ice, brandy, lemon juice, orange syrup and sugar syrup. Shake well, pour into a tumbler and top up with ginger ale.

GEORGIA MINT JULEP

GRASSHOPPER

25 ML/1 FL OZ CRÈME DE CACAO
25 ML/1 FL OZ GREEN CRÈME DE MENTHE

Pour crème de cacao into a pousse-café glass.
Add crème de menthe, pouring it gently over
back of spoon so that it floats on surface. Serve
with a straw.

HONEYMOON

2–3 ICE CUBES
25 ML/1 FL OZ CALVADOS
15 ML/½ FL OZ BÉNÉDICTINE
10 ML/2 TEASPOONS ORANGE JUICE
3 DASHES COINTREAU

Crack ice and put in a shaker with other
ingredients. Shake and strain into a cocktail
glass.

GREENHORN

50 ML/2 FL OZ GREEN CRÈME DE MENTHE
20 ML/¾ FL OZ LEMON JUICE
2–3 ICE CUBES
MINERAL WATER

Put crème de menthe and lemon juice in a
shaker, and shake well. Put ice in a tumbler,
pour in contents of shaker and top up to taste
with mineral water.

INTERNATIONAL

2–3 ICE CUBES
20 ML/¾ FL OZ BRANDY
20 ML/¾ FL OZ GREEN CHARTREUSE
15 ML/½ FL OZ PINEAPPLE JUICE
1 LEMON WEDGE

Crack ice and put in a shaker with brandy,
Chartreuse and pineapple juice. Shake very well
and strain into a cocktail glass. Add lemon
wedge, and serve with a straw.

Island Highball

2 ICE CUBES
15 ML/½ FL OZ BRANDY
15 ML/½ FL OZ GIN
15 ML/½ FL OZ RED VERMOUTH
1 DASH ORANGE BITTERS
SODA WATER

Put ice in a tumbler with brandy, gin, vermouth and bitters. Stir and top up to taste with soda water. Serve with a straw.

Klondyke Cocktail

3 ICE CUBES
40 ML/1½ FL OZ CALVADOS
15 ML/½ FL OZ DRY VERMOUTH
1 DASH ANGOSTURA BITTERS
1 OLIVE
PIECE OF LEMON PEEL

Put ice in a mixing glass with Calvados, vermouth and bitters. Stir well and strain into a cocktail glass. Decorate with olive and squeeze lemon peel over top. Serve with a cocktail stick.

Kirsch Cobbler

4 ICE CUBES
40 ML/1½ FL OZ KIRSCH
40 ML/1½ FL OZ MARASCHINO
6–8 COCKTAIL CHERRIES
SODA WATER

Crush ice and put in a goblet. Add kirsch, maraschino and cherries. Stir and top up with soda water. Serve with a straw and spoon.

Lone Tree Cooler

2–3 ICE CUBES
40 ML/1½ FL OZ APRICOT BRANDY
25 ML/1 FL OZ LEMON JUICE
20 ML/¾ FL OZ LIME JUICE
1 DASH GRENADINE
1 DASH ANGOSTURA BITTERS
SODA WATER

Crush ice and put in a shaker with all other ingredients except soda water. Shake and pour into a tall stemmed glass. Top up with soda water and serve with a straw.

MORNING GLORY AND MORNING GLORY FIZZ (page 68)

MORNING GLORY

2–3 ICE CUBES
20 ML/¾ FL OZ BRANDY
20 ML/¾ FL OZ BOURBON WHISKY
10 ML/2 TEASPOONS SUGAR SYRUP
2 DASHES COINTREAU
1 DASH PERNOD
SODA WATER
SPIRAL OF LEMON PEEL

Put ice in a mixing glass with brandy, whisky, sugar syrup, Cointreau and Pernod. Stir well and strain into a small tumbler or balloon glass. Top up with soda water, and stir. Decorate with spiral of lemon peel.

NORMAN FERRY

ICE CUBES
25 ML/1 FL OZ CALVADOS
25 ML/1 FL OZ LIME CORDIAL
GINGER BEER
SQUEEZE OF FRESH LIME
1 SLICE OF LIME
1 SLICE OF LEMON

Crush ice and put in a tall tumbler. Add Calvados and lime cordial, and top up with ginger beer. Add a squeeze of fresh lime, and decorate with slices of lime and lemon.

NATASHA

2–3 ICE CUBES
15 ML/½ FL OZ APRICOT BRANDY
15 ML/½ FL OZ PEAR BRANDY
15 ML/½ FL OZ RED VERMOUTH
1 DASH ORANGE BITTERS
1 COCKTAIL CHERRY

Put ice in a mixing glass with apricot brandy, pear brandy, vermouth and bitters. Stir and strain into a cocktail glass. Decorate with cherry.

PRINCE OF WALES

2–3 ICE CUBES
15 ML/½ FL OZ BRANDY
15 ML/½ FL OZ COINTREAU
1 DASH ANGOSTURA BITTERS
SPARKLING WINE
½ LEMON SLICE

Crack ice and put in a shaker with brandy, Cointreau and bitters. Shake well and strain into a tall champagne glass. Top up with sparkling wine, and fix lemon slice on rim of glass.

NATASHA

21

QUEEN MARY

2–3 ICE CUBES
25 ML/1 FL OZ BRANDY
25 ML/1 FL OZ COINTREAU
2 DASHES STRAWBERRY SYRUP
1 DASH PERNOD
1 STRAWBERRY

Crack ice and put in a shaker with brandy, Cointreau, strawberry syrup and Pernod. Shake well and strain into a cocktail glass. Decorate with strawberry, and serve with a cocktail stick.

SANTA FÉ EXPRESS

2–3 ICE CUBES
15 ML/½ FL OZ COINTREAU
5 ML/1 TEASPOON LEMON JUICE
40 ML/1½ FL OZ ORANGE JUICE
SODA WATER
10–12 FROZEN RASPBERRIES

Put ice, Cointreau and lemon juice in a large cocktail glass, and stir. Top up with orange juice and soda water. Add raspberries, still frozen, spearing a few of them on a cocktail stick.

RITZ

2–3 ICE CUBES
25 ML/1 FL OZ BRANDY
15 ML/½ FL OZ COINTREAU
15 ML/½ FL OZ ORANGE JUICE
CHAMPAGNE

Crack ice and put in a shaker with brandy, Cointreau and orange juice. Shake well and strain into a tall champagne glass. Top up with champagne.

SIDECAR

2–3 ICE CUBES
25 ML/1 FL OZ BRANDY
15 ML/½ FL OZ COINTREAU
15 ML/½ FL OZ LEMON JUICE
1 COCKTAIL CHERRY

Crack ice and put in a shaker with brandy, Cointreau and lemon juice. Shake and strain into a cocktail glass. Spear cherry on a cocktail stick and use to decorate.

STINGER

2–3 ICE CUBES
25 ML/1 FL OZ BRANDY
25 ML/1 FL OZ GREEN CRÈME DE MENTHE

Crack ice and put in a shaker with brandy and
crème de menthe. Shake and strain into a
cocktail glass.

TOSCANINI

3–4 ICE CUBES
25 ML/1 FL OZ CORDIAL MÉDOC
15 ML/½ FL OZ COINTREAU
15 ML/½ FL OZ BRANDY
CHAMPAGNE

Crack ice and put in a shaker with Cordial
Médoc, Cointreau and brandy. Shake well and
strain into a tall champagne glass. Top up with
champagne.

SWEET LADY

2–3 ICE CUBES
25 ML/1 FL OZ CRÈME DE CACAO
15 ML/½ FL OZ WHISKY
15 ML/½ FL OZ PEACH BRANDY

Crack ice and put in a shaker with other
ingredients. Shake well and strain into a cocktail
glass.

ZOOM

2–3 ICE CUBES
40 ML/1½ FL OZ BRANDY
20 ML/¾ FL OZ CREAM
15 ML/½ FL OZ HONEY

Crack ice and put in a shaker with other
ingredients. Shake well and strain into a large
cocktail glass.

ALASKA

GIN-BASED COCKTAILS

ALASKA

40 ML/1½ FL OZ GIN
15 ML/½ FL OZ YELLOW CHARTREUSE

Put the ingredients in a shaker and shake well.
Strain into a cocktail glass.

ANGEL'S FACE

2–3 ICE CUBES
20 ML/¾ FL OZ GIN
20 ML/¾ FL OZ APRICOT BRANDY
10 ML/2 TEASPOONS CALVADOS

Crack ice and put in a shaker with other
ingredients. Shake well and strain into a cocktail
glass.

BERLIN

3 ICE CUBES
20 ML/¾ FL OZ GIN
20 ML/¾ FL OZ MADEIRA
20 ML/¾ FL OZ ORANGE JUICE
1 DASH ANGOSTURA BITTERS

Crush ice and put in a shaker with other
ingredients. Shake well and pour into a cocktail
glass. Serve with a straw.

BERLIN

BLOODHOUND

4 ICE CUBES
15 ML/½ FL OZ GIN
15 ML/½ FL OZ DRY VERMOUTH
15 ML/½ FL OZ RED VERMOUTH
2–3 DASHES STRAWBERRY LIQUEUR
4 STRAWBERRIES

Crack ice. Put half cracked ice in an electric blender with gin, vermouths, strawberry liqueur and two strawberries. Blend briefly and strain into a cocktail glass. Add remaining cracked ice and decorate with remaining strawberries. Serve with a straw and a spoon.

BRONX

2–3 ICE CUBES
15 ML/½ FL OZ GIN
15 ML/½ FL OZ DRY VERMOUTH
15 ML/½ FL OZ RED VERMOUTH
15 ML/½ FL OZ ORANGE JUICE
1 DASH ANGOSTURA BITTERS
SPIRAL OF ORANGE PEEL

Crack ice and put in a shaker with gin, vermouths, orange juice and bitters. Shake well and strain into a cocktail glass. Spear orange peel on a cocktail stick and use to decorate.

BLUE LADY

2–3 ICE CUBES
25 ML/1 FL OZ GIN
15 ML/½ FL OZ BLUE CURAÇAO
15 ML/½ FL OZ LEMON JUICE
1 COCKTAIL CHERRY

Crack ice and put in a shaker with gin, curaçao and lemon juice. Shake well and strain into a cocktail glass. Decorate with cherry.

CLOVER CLUB

2–3 ICE CUBES
1 EGG WHITE
15 ML/½ FL OZ LEMON JUICE
40 ML/1½ FL OZ GIN
20 ML/¾ FL OZ GRENADINE

Crack ice and put in a shaker with other ingredients. Shake very well and strain into a small goblet.

COOPERSTOWN

2–3 ICE CUBES
25 ML/1 FL OZ GIN
15 ML/½ FL OZ DRY VERMOUTH
15 ML/½ FL OZ BIANCO VERMOUTH
1 SPRIG OF MINT

Put ice in a mixing glass with gin and vermouths.
Stir well and strain into a cocktail glass.
Decorate with sprig of mint.

EMPIRE

2–3 ICE CUBES
25 ML/1 FL OZ GIN
15 ML/½ FL OZ CALVADOS
15 ML/½ FL OZ APRICOT BRANDY
2 COCKTAIL CHERRIES

Put ice in a mixing glass with gin, Calvados and
apricot brandy. Stir well and strain into a
cocktail glass. Decorate with cherries and serve
with a cocktail stick.

DERBY

40 ML/1½ FL OZ GIN
15 ML/½ FL OZ PEACH BRANDY
1 SPRIG OF MINT

Chill gin and peach brandy, then pour into a
cocktail glass and stir. Decorate with sprig of
mint.

FRENCH COCKTAIL

2–3 ICE CUBES
25 ML/1 FL OZ GIN
20 ML/¾ FL OZ PERNOD
5 ML/1 TEASPOON GRENADINE

Crack ice and put in a shaker with other
ingredients. Shake and strain into a cocktail
glass.

ETON BLAZER

ETON BLAZER

3–4 ICE CUBES
25 ML/1 FL OZ GIN
25 ML/1 FL OZ KIRSCH
15 ML/½ FL OZ LEMON JUICE
10 ML/2 TEASPOONS SUGAR SYRUP
SODA WATER
2 COCKTAIL CHERRIES

Place ice, gin, kirsch, lemon juice and sugar syrup in a tumbler. Stir, then top up with soda water. Decorate with cherries.

GIMLET

2–3 ICE CUBES
50 ML/2 FL OZ GIN
25 ML/1 FL OZ LIME CORDIAL
SODA WATER

Put ice in a mixing glass with gin and lime cordial. Stir well and strain into a large cocktail glass. Add a shot of soda water.

Green Fizz

4–5 ICE CUBES
1 EGG WHITE
10 ML/2 TEASPOONS SUGAR SYRUP
25 ML/1 FL OZ LEMON JUICE
50 ML/2 FL OZ GIN
5 ML/1 TEASPOON GREEN CRÈME DE MENTHE
SODA WATER

Crack ice and put in a shaker with egg white, sugar syrup, lemon juice, gin and crème de menthe. Shake very well and strain into a tall glass. Top up with soda water and serve with a straw.

Green Hat

2–3 ICE CUBES
25 ML/1 FL OZ GIN
25 ML/1 FL OZ GREEN CRÈME DE MENTHE
SODA WATER

Put ice in a large goblet or tumbler with gin and crème de menthe. Stir and top up with soda water. Serve with a straw.

GREEN FIZZ

29

GIN OYSTER

5 ML/1 TEASPOON GIN
1 EGG YOLK
10 ML/2 TEASPOONS TOMATO KETCHUP
1 DASH WORCESTERSHIRE SAUCE
1 DASH LEMON JUICE
SALT, PEPPER, PAPRIKA, NUTMEG

Put gin in a shallow glass. Slide in egg yolk. Add tomato ketchup, Worcestershire sauce and lemon juice. Sprinkle with salt, pepper and paprika, and grate over a little nutmeg. Do not stir this drink, but swallow it in one gulp.

GIN SLING

2–3 ICE CUBES
40 ML/1½ FL OZ GIN
20 ML/¾ FL OZ LEMON JUICE
10 ML/2 TEASPOONS CASTER SUGAR
1 DASH ANGOSTURA BITTERS
MINERAL WATER

Put ice in a tumbler with gin, lemon juice, sugar and bitters. Stir and top up with mineral water.

GIN PUNCH

3 ICE CUBES
40 ML/1½ FL OZ GIN
15 ML/½ FL OZ LEMON JUICE
10 ML/2 TEASPOONS CASTER SUGAR
2 DASHES MARASCHINO
3–4 COCKTAIL CHERRIES
3–4 PINEAPPLE CHUNKS

Crush ice and put in a shallow tumbler. Add gin, lemon juice, sugar and maraschino. Stir, then decorate with cherries and pineapple chunks. Serve with a straw and a spoon.

HAWAII KISS

1 PINEAPPLE
25 ML/1 FL OZ GIN
2 ICE CUBES
SPARKLING WINE

Scoop out flesh from pineapple, press juice out of flesh and return juice to hollowed-out shell. Add gin and ice, and top up with sparkling wine. Serve with straws.

Serves 2

HORSE'S NECK

SPIRAL OF LEMON PEEL
ICE CUBES
50 ML/2 FL OZ GIN
DRY GINGER ALE

Place one end of lemon peel over edge of a
tumbler, allowing remainder to curl inside.
Anchor with two ice cubes. Add gin and top up
with ginger ale.

LADY BROWN

2–3 ICE CUBES
40 ML/1½ FL OZ GIN
20 ML/¾ FL OZ GRAND MARNIER
20 ML/¾ FL OZ MANDARIN ORANGE JUICE
15 ML/½ FL OZ LEMON JUICE
2 MANDARIN ORANGE SEGMENTS

Crack ice and put in a shaker with gin, Grand
Marnier, mandarin orange juice and lemon
juice. Shake very well. Place mandarin orange
segments in a large cocktail glass, strain in
contents of shaker and serve with a straw.

JOHN COLLINS

2–3 ICE CUBES
25 ML/1 FL OZ GIN
15 ML/½ FL OZ LEMON JUICE
10 ML/2 TEASPOONS CASTER SUGAR
SODA WATER

Put ice in a tumbler with gin, lemon juice and
sugar. Top up with soda water, and stir.

MAGNOLIA BLOSSOM

2–3 ICE CUBES
25 ML/1 FL OZ GIN
15 ML/½ FL OZ CREAM
10 ML/2 TEASPOONS LEMON JUICE
2 DASHES GRENADINE

Crack ice and put in a shaker with other
ingredients. Shake and strain into a cocktail
glass. Serve with a straw.

MONTE CARLO IMPERIAL AND
MONTE CARLO COCKTAIL (page 67)

MAIDEN

2–3 ICE CUBES
25 ML/1 FL OZ ORANGE JUICE
20 ML/¾ FL OZ GIN
20 ML/¾ FL OZ COINTREAU
15 ML/½ FL OZ LEMON JUICE

Crack ice and put in a shaker with other
ingredients. Shake well and strain into a large
cocktail glass.

MONTE CARLO
IMPERIAL

2–3 ICE CUBES
25 ML/1 FL OZ GIN
15 ML/½ FL OZ WHITE CRÈME DE MENTHE
10 ML/2 TEASPOONS LIME JUICE
CHAMPAGNE

Crack ice and put in a shaker with gin, crème de
menthe and lime juice. Shake and strain into a
tall champagne glass. Top up with champagne.

MOULIN ROUGE

2–3 ICE CUBES
25 ML/1 FL OZ GIN
20 ML/¾ FL OZ APRICOT BRANDY
20 ML/¾ FL OZ LEMON JUICE
5 ML/1 TEASPOON GRENADINE
SPARKLING WINE
1 ORANGE SLICE

Crack ice and put in a shaker with gin, apricot brandy, lemon juice and grenadine. Shake and strain into a shallow champagne glass. Top up with sparkling wine, and decorate with orange slice. Serve with a straw.

MARTINI DRY

2–3 ICE CUBES
50 ML/2 FL OZ GIN
10 ML/2 TEASPOONS DRY VERMOUTH
PIECE OF LEMON PEEL
1 OLIVE (OPTIONAL)

Put ice in a mixing glass with gin and vermouth, and stir well. Strain into a cocktail glass and squeeze lemon peel over top. If liked, spear olive on a cocktail stick and use to decorate.

MOULIN ROUGE

33

Martini Medium

2–3 ICE CUBES
40 ML/1½ FL OZ GIN
10 ML/2 TEASPOONS DRY VERMOUTH
10 ML/2 TEASPOONS RED VERMOUTH
PIECE OF ORANGE PEEL

Put ice in a mixing glass with gin and vermouths.
Stir well and strain into a cocktail glass.
Decorate with orange peel.

Martini Sweet

2–3 ICE CUBES
40 ML/1½ FL OZ GIN
15 ML/½ FL OZ RED VERMOUTH
5 ML/1 TEASPOON SUGAR SYRUP or GRENADINE
1 COCKTAIL CHERRY

Put ice in a mixing glass with gin, vermouth and
sugar syrup or grenadine. Stir well and strain into
a cocktail glass. Decorate with cherry and serve
with a cocktail stick.

Martini on the Rocks

2–3 ICE CUBES
50 ML/2 FL OZ GIN
5 ML/1 TEASPOON DRY VERMOUTH
1 LEMON SLICE

Put ice in a small tumbler with gin and
vermouth. Stir, then decorate with lemon
slice.

Mule's Hind Leg

2–3 ICE CUBES
15 ML/½ FL OZ GIN
15 ML/½ FL OZ CALVADOS
15 ML/½ FL OZ BÉNÉDICTINE
15 ML/½ FL OZ APRICOT BRANDY
10 ML/2 TEASPOONS MAPLE SYRUP

Put ice in a mixing glass with other ingredients.
Stir well and strain into a cocktail glass.

NEGRONI

3 ICE CUBES
25 ML/1 FL OZ GIN
15 ML/½ FL OZ CAMPARI
15 ML/½ FL OZ RED VERMOUTH
SODA WATER
1 ORANGE SLICE

Put ice in a tall tumbler. Add gin, Campari and vermouth, and top up with soda water. Decorate with orange slice and serve with a straw.

PINK GIN

3–4 ICE CUBES
50 ML/2 FL OZ GIN
3 DASHES ANGOSTURA BITTERS

Put ice in a mixing glass with gin and bitters. Stir and strain into a cocktail glass.

OPERA

2–3 ICE CUBES
25 ML/1 FL OZ GIN
15 ML/½ FL OZ DUBONNET
15 ML/½ FL OZ MARASCHINO
PIECE OF ORANGE PEEL

Crack ice and put in a shaker with gin, Dubonnet and maraschino. Shake well and strain into a cocktail glass. Squeeze orange peel over top.

PINK LADY FIZZ

2–3 ICE CUBES
1 EGG WHITE
10 ML/2 TEASPOONS GRENADINE
25 ML/1 FL OZ LEMON JUICE
50 ML/2 FL OZ GIN
SODA WATER

Crack ice and put in a shaker with egg white, grenadine, lemon juice and gin. Shake very well and strain into a goblet. Top up with soda water and serve with a straw.

FROM LEFT TO RIGHT: QUEEN BEE, QUEEN ELIZABETH,
QUEEN MARY (page 22), QUEEN'S PEG AND QUEEN'S COCKTAIL

Queen Bee

2–3 ICE CUBES
25 ML/1 FL OZ SLOE GIN
25 ML/1 FL OZ COINTREAU
1 DASH PERNOD

Crack ice and put in a shaker with other ingredients. Shake well and strain into a cocktail glass.

Queen's Cocktail

4 PINEAPPLE CHUNKS
2–3 ICE CUBES
25 ML/1 FL OZ GIN
15 ML/½ FL OZ BIANCO VERMOUTH
15 ML/½ FL OZ DRY VERMOUTH

Put pineapple chunks in a mixing glass and crush with a spoon. Add other ingredients and stir well. Strain into a cocktail glass.

Queen Elizabeth

2–3 ICE CUBES
25 ML/1 FL OZ GIN
15 ML/½ FL OZ COINTREAU
15 ML/½ FL OZ LEMON JUICE
1 DASH PERNOD
1 COCKTAIL CHERRY

Crack ice and put in a shaker with gin, Cointreau, lemon juice and Pernod. Shake well and strain into a cocktail glass. Decorate with cherry.

Queen's Peg

1 LARGE ICE CUBE
25 ML/1 FL OZ GIN
SPARKLING WINE

Put ice in a goblet, add gin and top up with sparkling wine.

Ramona Cocktail

1 SPRIG OF MINT
2–3 ICE CUBES
25 ML/1 FL OZ GIN
25 ML/1 FL OZ LEMON JUICE
2 DASHES GRENADINE

Coarsely chop mint. Crack ice and put in a shaker with mint and other ingredients. Shake well and strain into a cocktail glass.

Rose

15 ML/½ FL OZ LEMON JUICE
15 ML/1 TABLESPOON CASTER SUGAR
3 ICE CUBES
25 ML/1 FL OZ GIN
15 ML/½ FL OZ APRICOT BRANDY
15 ML/½ FL OZ DRY VERMOUTH
1 DASH GRENADINE
1 COCKTAIL CHERRY

Dip rim of a cocktail glass first in lemon juice, shaking off excess, then in sugar. Allow frosting to dry. Put ice in a mixing glass with gin, apricot brandy, vermouth, grenadine and a dash of remaining lemon juice. Stir and strain into cocktail glass. Decorate with cherry.

Rolls-Royce

2–3 ICE CUBES
25 ML/1 FL OZ GIN
15 ML/½ FL OZ DRY VERMOUTH
15 ML/½ FL OZ BIANCO VERMOUTH
1–2 DASHES BÉNÉDICTINE
1 COCKTAIL CHERRY

Put ice in a mixing glass with gin, vermouths and Bénédictine. Stir well and strain into a cocktail glass. Decorate with cherry and serve with a cocktail stick.

Sake Special

2–3 ICE CUBES
50 ML/2 FL OZ GIN
25 ML/1 FL OZ SAKE
2 DASHES ANGOSTURA BITTERS

Put ice in a mixing glass with other ingredients. Stir well and strain into a cocktail glass.

SILVER STREAK

ICE CUBES
40 ML/1½ FL OZ DRY GIN
25 ML/1 FL OZ KÜMMEL

Put ice cubes in a cocktail glass and pour gin and kümmel over them.

TAKE TWO

2–3 ICE CUBES
25 ML/1 FL OZ GIN
15 ML/½ FL OZ COINTREAU
10 ML/2 TEASPOONS CAMPARI

Put ice in a mixing glass with other ingredients. Stir well and strain into a cocktail glass.

SINGAPORE GIN SLING

2–3 ICE CUBES
50 ML/2 FL OZ GIN
25 ML/1 FL OZ LEMON JUICE
15 ML/½ FL OZ CHERRY BRANDY
15 ML/½ FL OZ COINTREAU
10 ML/2 TEASPOONS CASTER SUGAR
SODA WATER
1 LEMON SLICE

Put ice in a tall glass with gin, lemon juice, cherry brandy, Cointreau and sugar. Stir and top up with soda water. Decorate with lemon slice.

WHITE LADY

2–3 ICE CUBES
½ EGG WHITE
10 ML/2 TEASPOONS LEMON JUICE
25 ML/1 FL OZ GIN
10 ML/2 TEASPOONS COINTREAU
1 COCKTAIL CHERRY

Crack ice and put in a shaker with egg white, lemon juice, gin and Cointreau. Shake very well and strain into a cocktail glass. Spear cherry on a cocktail stick and use to decorate.

Bacardi Blossom

Rum-based Cocktails

Bacardi Blossom

2–3 ICE CUBES
40 ML/1½ FL OZ BACARDI RUM
10 ML/2 TEASPOONS ORANGE JUICE
10 ML/2 TEASPOONS LEMON JUICE
5 ML/1 TEASPOON SUGAR SYRUP

Crack ice and put in a shaker with other ingredients. Shake well and strain into a cocktail glass.

BACARDI HIGHBALL

3 ICE CUBES
25 ML/1 FL OZ BACARDI RUM
25 ML/1 FL OZ COINTREAU
5 ML/1 TEASPOON LEMON JUICE
SODA WATER

Crack two ice cubes and put in a shaker. Add rum, Cointreau and lemon juice. Shake well and strain into a goblet or glass mug. Add remaining ice cube and a shot of soda water. Serve with a straw.

BANANA DAIQUIRI

ICE CUBES
25 ML/1 FL OZ WHITE RUM
25 ML/1 FL OZ SINGLE CREAM
25 ML/1 FL OZ BANANA LIQUEUR
½ BANANA

Crush ice and put in a blender with other ingredients. Blend well, then pour into a cocktail glass.

BACARDI HIGHBALL

41

BLUE HAWAIIAN

ICE CUBES
15 ML/½ FL OZ RUM
15 ML/½ FL OZ BLUE CURAÇAO
25 ML/1 FL OZ SINGLE CREAM
50 ML/2 FL OZ COCONUT CREAM
100 ML/4 FL OZ PINEAPPLE JUICE
1 SLICE FRESH PINEAPPLE
1 COCKTAIL CHERRY

Crush ice and put all ingredients, apart from the fresh pineapple, in a blender. Blend well, then pour into a tall tumbler. Decorate with pineapple slice. Spear cherry on a cocktail stick and attach to pineapple.

CUBA CRUSTA

15 ML/½ FL OZ LEMON JUICE
15 ML/1 TABLESPOON CASTER SUGAR
2–3 ICE CUBES
40 ML/1½ FL OZ WHITE RUM
10 ML/2 TEASPOONS PINEAPPLE JUICE
5 ML/1 TEASPOON COINTREAU
SPIRAL OF LEMON PEEL

Dip rim of a goblet first in lemon juice, shaking off excess, then in sugar. Allow frosting to dry. Crack ice and put in a shaker with rum, pineapple juice, Cointreau and remaining lemon juice. Shake and strain into glass. Decorate with spiral of lemon peel.

COLUMBUS

2–3 ICE CUBES
20 ML/¾ FL OZ RUM
20 ML/¾ FL OZ APRICOT BRANDY
20 ML/¾ FL OZ LIME JUICE

Crack ice and put in a shaker with other ingredients. Shake well and strain into a cocktail glass.

CUBA LIBRE

2–3 ICE CUBES
50 ML/2 FL OZ WHITE RUM
15 ML/½ FL OZ LEMON JUICE
COCA-COLA
1 LEMON SLICE

Put ice in a tall tumbler with rum and lemon juice. Top up with Coca-Cola, and stir. Fix lemon slice on rim of glass and serve with a straw.

DAIQUIRI AMERICAN-STYLE

5–6 ICE CUBES
50 ML/2 FL OZ WHITE RUM
25 ML/1 FL OZ LIME JUICE
5 ML/1 TEASPOON COINTREAU
5 ML/1 TEASPOON SUGAR SYRUP
1 LEMON or LIME SLICE
1 COCKTAIL CHERRY

Crack two ice cubes and put in an electric blender with rum, lime juice, Cointreau and sugar syrup. Blend. Crush remaining ice and put in a goblet. Strain contents of blender over crushed ice. Decorate with lemon or lime slice and cherry, and serve with a straw.

DAWN CRUSTA

15 ML/½ FL OZ LEMON JUICE
15 ML/1 TABLESPOON CASTER SUGAR
2–3 ICE CUBES
40 ML/1½ FL OZ WHITE RUM
15 ML/½ FL OZ ORANGE JUICE
5 ML/1 TEASPOON APRICOT BRANDY
1 DASH GRENADINE
SPIRAL OF ORANGE PEEL

Dip rim of a cocktail glass first in lemon juice, shaking off excess, then in sugar. Allow frosting to dry. Crack ice and put in a shaker with rum, orange juice, apricot brandy and grenadine. Shake and strain into glass. Decorate with spiral of orange peel.

DAIQUIRI ON THE ROCKS

6–7 ICE CUBES
50 ML/2 FL OZ WHITE RUM
25 ML/1 FL OZ LIME JUICE
15 ML/½ FL OZ SUGAR SYRUP

Crack two ice cubes and put in a shaker with rum, lime juice and sugar syrup. Shake very well. Put remaining ice in a tumbler, and strain in contents of shaker. Serve with a straw.

EL DORADO

2–3 ICE CUBES
25 ML/1 FL OZ WHITE RUM
25 ML/1 FL OZ ADVOCAAT
25 ML/1 FL OZ CRÈME DE CACAO
5 ML/1 TEASPOON GRATED COCONUT

Crack ice and put in a shaker with other ingredients. Shake very well and strain into a large cocktail glass. Serve with a straw.

EAST INDIA

EAST INDIA

2 ICE CUBES
40 ML/1½ FL OZ WHITE RUM
5 ML/1 TEASPOON COINTREAU
5 ML/1 TEASPOON PINEAPPLE JUICE
1 DASH ANGOSTURA BITTERS
1 COCKTAIL CHERRY

Crack ice and put in a shaker with rum,
Cointreau, pineapple juice and bitters. Shake
and strain into a cocktail glass. Decorate with
cherry and serve with a cocktail stick.

GOOD MORNING

2–3 ICE CUBES
1 EGG WHITE
5 ML/1 TEASPOON SUGAR SYRUP
15 ML/½ FL OZ LEMON JUICE
20 ML/¾ FL OZ RUM
20 ML/¾ FL OZ PORT

Crack ice and put in a shaker with other
ingredients. Shake very well and strain into a
small tumbler. Serve with a straw.

FIREMAN'S SOUR

2–3 ICE CUBES
80 ML/3 FL OZ WHITE RUM
15 ML/½ FL OZ LEMON JUICE
5 ML/1 TEASPOON GRENADINE
6 SMALL TRIANGLES OF LEMON
3 COCKTAIL CHERRIES
SODA WATER

Crack ice and put in a shaker with rum, lemon juice and grenadine. Shake well and strain into a tumbler. Decorate with small triangles of lemon and with cherries. Top up with a little soda water.

FIREMAN'S SOUR

HAVANA CLUB

2–3 ICE CUBES
40 ML/1½ FL OZ WHITE RUM
20 ML/¾ FL OZ RED VERMOUTH
1 COCKTAIL CHERRY

Crack ice and put in a shaker with rum and vermouth. Shake well and strain into a cocktail glass. Spear cherry on a cocktail stick and use to decorate.

HEMINGWAY

2–3 ICE CUBES
40 ML/1½ FL OZ WHITE RUM
40 ML/1½ FL OZ COINTREAU
40 ML/1½ FL OZ GRAPEFRUIT JUICE
SPARKLING WINE

Crack ice and put in a shaker with rum, Cointreau and grapefruit juice. Shake very well and strain into a champagne glss. Top up with sparkling wine and serve with a straw.

HORSE GUARDS

2–3 ICE CUBES
1 EGG YOLK
20 ML/¾ FL OZ RUM
20 ML/¾ FL OZ COINTREAU
SPARKLING WINE
SPIRAL OF LEMON PEEL

Crack ice and put in a shaker with egg yolk, rum and Cointreau. Shake very well and strain into a tumbler. Top up with sparkling wine and decorate with spiral of lemon peel. Serve with a straw.

PINA COLADA

ICE CUBES
25 ML/1 FL OZ WHITE RUM
25 ML/1 FL OZ SINGLE CREAM
50 ML/2 FL OZ COCONUT CREAM
100 ML/4 FL OZ PINEAPPLE JUICE
1 PIECE FRESH PINEAPPLE
1 COCKTAIL CHERRY

Crush ice and put all ingredients, apart from pineapple and cherry, in a blender. Blend well, then pour into a tall tumbler. Decorate glass with pineapple. Spear cherry on to a cocktail stick and attach to pineapple.

MAI TAI

50 ML/2 FL OZ WHITE RUM
25 ML/1 FL OZ ORANGE JUICE
25 ML/1 FL OZ LIME JUICE
3 ICE CUBES
3 COCKTAIL CHERRIES
3 PINEAPPLE CHUNKS
2 ORANGE SLICES

Put rum, orange juice and lime juice in a small goblet and stir well. Crush ice and add to glass. Decorate with cherries, pineapple chunks and orange slices. Serve with a straw and a spoon.

PRESIDENTE

3–4 ICE CUBES
40 ML/1½ FL OZ WHITE RUM
25 ML/1 FL OZ DRY VERMOUTH
SPIRAL OF ORANGE PEEL

Put ice in a mixing glass with rum and vermouth. Stir very well and pour into a small goblet. Decorate with spiral of orange peel.

Quarter Deck

2–3 ICE CUBES
40 ML/1½ FL OZ DARK RUM
15 ML/½ FL OZ SHERRY
10 ML/2 TEASPOONS LIME JUICE

Crack ice and put in a shaker with other ingredients. Shake very well and strain into a cocktail glass.

Redskin

2–3 ICE CUBES
50 ML/2 FL OZ WHITE RUM
10 ML/2 TEASPOONS GRENADINE
PEPPER, CINNAMON, NUTMEG
1 LEMON SLICE

Crack ice and put in a shaker with rum and grenadine. Add pepper, ground cinnamon and grated nutmeg. Shake and strain into a cocktail glass. Fix lemon slice on rim of glass to decorate.

Ramona Fizz

2–3 ICE CUBES
50 ML/2 FL OZ WHITE RUM
50 ML/2 FL OZ LEMON JUICE
25 ML/1 FL OZ COINTREAU
10 ML/2 TEASPOONS CASTER SUGAR
SODA WATER
1 LEMON SLICE

Crack ice and put in a shaker with rum, lemon juice, Cointreau and sugar. Shake very well and strain into a tall tumbler. Top up with soda water and fix lemon slice on rim of glass. Serve with a straw.

Rocky Mountains Punch

2–3 ICE CUBES
25 ML/1 FL OZ RUM
15 ML/½ FL OZ LEMON JUICE
10 ML/2 TEASPOONS MARASCHINO
2–3 PINEAPPLE CHUNKS
1–2 CHERRIES
SPARKLING WINE

Crack ice and put in a shaker with rum, lemon juice and maraschino. Shake and strain into a goblet. Decorate with fruits and top up with sparkling wine. Serve with a straw and a spoon.

PLANTER'S COCKTAIL

2–3 ICE CUBES
40 ML/1½ FL OZ RUM
20 ML/¾ FL OZ ORANGE JUICE
20 ML/¾ FL OZ LEMON JUICE
2 DASHES ANGOSTURA BITTERS
5 ML/1 TEASPOON CASTER SUGAR
3 PINEAPPLE CHUNKS
1 COCKTAIL CHERRY

Crack ice and put in a shaker with rum, orange juice, lemon juice, bitters and sugar. Shake very well and strain into a large cocktail glass. Decorate with pineapple chunks and cherry, and serve with a cocktail stick.

PLANTER'S COCKTAIL

PLANTER'S PUNCH

4–6 ICE CUBES
50 ML/2 FL OZ WHITE RUM
15 ML/½ FL OZ LEMON JUICE
10 ML/2 TEASPOONS SUGAR SYRUP
1 ORANGE SLICE
1 COCKTAIL CHERRY
1 STRAWBERRY
2 RASPBERRIES

Crack half ice and put in a shaker with rum, lemon juice and sugar syrup. Shake well. Crush remaining ice and put in a tall tumbler. Pour in contents of shaker and stir. Decorate with orange slice, cherry, strawberry and raspberries. Serve with a straw and a spoon.

Rum Alexander

2–3 ICE CUBES
25 ML/1 FL OZ CRÈME DE CACAO
15 ML/½ FL OZ WHITE RUM
15 ML/½ FL OZ CREAM

Crack ice and put in a shaker with other ingredients. Shake well and strain into a cocktail glass.

Rum Cocktail

25 ML/1 FL OZ WHITE RUM
1 DASH ANGOSTURA BITTERS
5 ML/1 TEASPOON SUGAR SYRUP
2 ICE CUBES
SPIRAL OF ORANGE PEEL
PIECE OF ORANGE PEEL

Put rum, bitters and sugar syrup in a cocktail glass, and stir well. Add ice and decorate with spiral of orange peel. Squeeze remaining piece of orange peel over top.

RUM COCKTAIL

Rum Cobbler

3–4 ICE CUBES
5 ML/1 TEASPOON MARASCHINO
5 ML/1 TEASPOON GRENADINE
1 ORANGE SLICE
1 LIME SLICE
2 COCKTAIL CHERRIES
3–4 PINEAPPLE CHUNKS
1–2 STRAWBERRIES
RUM

Crush ice and put in a tall goblet. Add maraschino and grenadine. Decorate with fruits and top up with rum to taste. Serve with a straw and a spoon.

Rum Sour

2–3 ICE CUBES
40 ML/1½ FL OZ WHITE RUM
15 ML/½ FL OZ LEMON JUICE
5 ML/1 TEASPOON SUGAR SYRUP
2 COCKTAIL CHERRIES
2 LEMON SEGMENTS
SODA WATER

Crack ice and put in a shaker with rum, lemon juice and sugar syrup. Shake well and strain into a shallow champagne glass. Decorate with cherries and lemon segments and top up with soda water. Serve with a cocktail stick.

Rum Flip

2–3 ICE CUBES
1 EGG YOLK
10 ML/2 TEASPOONS SUGAR SYRUP
25 ML/1 FL OZ RUM
25 ML/1 FL OZ STRONG COLD TEA
10 ML/2 TEASPOONS COINTREAU

Crack ice and put in a shaker with other ingredients. Shake very well and strain into a flip glass. Serve with a straw.

Stingray

ICE CUBES
25 ML/1 FL OZ DARK RUM
4 LARGE FRESH STRAWBERRIES
1 DASH FRESH LEMON JUICE
1 DASH STRAWBERRY LIQUEUR or SYRUP

Crush ice and blend with the other ingredients. Pour into a cocktail glass.

SUMMERTIME

3 ICE CUBES
25 ML/1 FL OZ RUM
25 ML/1 FL OZ COINTREAU
10 ML/2 TEASPOONS GRENADINE
10 ML/2 TEASPOONS ORANGE JUICE
10 ML/2 TEASPOONS LEMON JUICE

Put ice in a mixing glass with other ingredients.
Stir well and strain into a large cocktail glass.

WAVE OF SYLT

15 ML/1 TABLESPOON CASTER SUGAR
50 ML/2 FL OZ BOILING WATER
25 ML/1 FL OZ RUM
25 ML/1 FL OZ RED WINE
1 CLOVE
NUTMEG
1 LEMON SLICE

Put sugar in a warmed flameproof punch glass.
Add boiling water and stir until sugar has
dissolved. Put rum, red wine and clove in a pan,
heat until just below boiling point, then pour
into glass. Grate a little nutmeg over top and
decorate with lemon slice.

THIRD RAIL

2–3 ICE CUBES
25 ML/1 FL OZ RUM
10 ML/2 TEASPOONS DRY VERMOUTH
10 ML/2 TEASPOONS RED VERMOUTH
10 ML/2 TEASPOONS ORANGE JUICE

Crack ice and put in a shaker with other
ingredients. Shake well and strain into a cocktail
glass.

XYZ

2–3 ICE CUBES
25 ML/1 FL OZ DARK RUM
15 ML/½ FL OZ COINTREAU
15 ML/½ FL OZ LEMON JUICE

Crack ice and put in a shaker with other
ingredients. Shake and strain into a cocktail
glass.

VODKA AND TEQUILA-BASED COCKTAILS

ACAPULCO

ACAPULCO

4 ICE CUBES
50 ML/2 FL OZ TEQUILA
25 ML/1 FL OZ CRÈME DE CASSIS
5 ML/1 TEASPOON SUGAR SYRUP
1 LEMON SLICE
SODA WATER

Crush ice and put in a balloon glass. Add tequila, crème de cassis and sugar syrup, and stir well. Add lemon slice and top up with soda water.

Blue Monday Nightcap (1)

2–3 ICE CUBES
25 ML/1 FL OZ VODKA
15 ML/½ FL OZ BLUE CURAÇAO
15 ML/½ FL OZ COINTREAU

Crack ice and put in a shaker with other ingredients. Shake well and strain into a tall glass.

Blue Monday Nightcap (2)

3 ICE CUBES
40 ML/1½ FL OZ VODKA
15 ML/½ FL OZ COINTREAU

Put ice in a mixing glass with vodka and Cointreau. Stir well and pour into a large cocktail glass.

BLUE MONDAY NIGHTCAPS (1) AND (2)

BALALAIKA

2–3 ICE CUBES
40 ML/1½ FL OZ VODKA
15 ML/½ FL OZ COINTREAU
15 ML/½ FL OZ LEMON JUICE
SPIRAL OF ORANGE PEEL

Crack ice and put in a shaker with vodka,
Cointreau and lemon juice. Shake well and
strain into a large cocktail glass. Decorate with
spiral of orange peel.

BLOODY MARY

25 ML/1 FL OZ VODKA
50 ML/2 FL OZ TOMATO JUICE
15 ML/½ FL OZ LEMON JUICE
2 DASHES WORCESTERSHIRE SAUCE
1 ICE CUBE (OPTIONAL)

Put vodka, tomato juice, lemon juice and
Worcestershire sauce in a tumbler and stir.
Crush ice, if using, and add to cocktail.

BLACK RUSSIAN

2–3 ICE CUBES
40 ML/1½ FL OZ VODKA
15 ML/½ FL OZ COFFEE LIQUEUR

Put ice in a mixing glass with vodka and coffee
liqueur. Stir well and pour into a tumbler.

BLUE DAY

2–3 ICE CUBES
40 ML/1½ FL OZ VODKA
20 ML/¾ FL OZ BLUE CURAÇAO
PEEL ½ LEMON
1 LEMON SLICE

Crack ice and put in a shaker with vodka and
curaçao. Shake well. Squeeze lemon peel over a
cocktail glass. Strain in contents of shaker and
fix lemon slice on rim of glass.

BULLSHOT

2–3 ICE CUBES
40 ML/1½ FL OZ VODKA
50 ML/2 FL OZ COLD BEEF CONSOMMÉ
SALT, PEPPER

Put ice in a mixing glass with other ingredients.
Stir and strain into a large cocktail glass.

GIPSY

2–3 ICE CUBES
25 ML/1 FL OZ VODKA
20 ML/¾ FL OZ BÉNÉDICTINE
1 DASH ANGOSTURA BITTERS

Crack ice and put in a shaker with other
ingredients. Shake and strain into a cocktail
glass.

EAST WIND

2–3 ICE CUBES
25 ML/1 FL OZ VODKA
15 ML/½ FL OZ DRY VERMOUTH
15 ML/½ FL OZ RED VERMOUTH
2–3 DASHES RUM

Crack ice and put in a shaker with other
ingredients. Shake and strain into a cocktail
glass.

GREEN DRAGON

2–3 ICE CUBES
40 ML/1½ FL OZ VODKA
40 ML/1½ FL OZ GREEN CRÈME DE MENTHE

Crack ice and put in a shaker with vodka and
crème de menthe. Shake and strain into a small
goblet.

GREEN HAT (page 29) AND GREEN SEA

GREEN SEA

2–3 ICE CUBES
25 ML/1 FL OZ VODKA
20 ML/¾ FL OZ DRY VERMOUTH
20 ML/¾ FL OZ GREEN CRÈME DE MENTHE

Crack ice and put in a shaker with other ingredients. Shake and strain into a small goblet.

LOUISA

3 FROZEN STUFFED OLIVES
40 ML/1½ FL OZ VODKA
65 ML/2½ FL OZ TOMATO JUICE
5 ML/1 TEASPOON LEMON JUICE
4 DASHES WORCESTERSHIRE SAUCE
SALT, PEPPER
SODA WATER

To prepare frozen stuffed olives, run a little water into the compartments of an ice tray, freeze, then add a stuffed olive to each compartment, fill up with water and freeze till hard. Place three frozen stuffed olives in a goblet. Add vodka, tomato juice, lemon juice, Worcestershire sauce, salt and pepper. Stir. Top up with soda water.

LOUISA

57

HARVEY WALLBANGER

4 ICE CUBES
50 ML/2 FL OZ VODKA
25 ML/1 FL OZ GALLIANO
25 ML/1 FL OZ ORANGE JUICE
2.5 ML/½ TEASPOON CASTER SUGAR
1 ORANGE SLICE

Crack two ice cubes and put in a shaker with vodka, Galliano, orange juice and sugar. Shake and strain into a tumbler. Add remaining ice and decorate with orange slice.

KAMIKAZE

ICE CUBES
25 ML/1 FL OZ VODKA
25 ML/1 FL OZ COINTREAU
25 ML/1 FL OZ LIME CORDIAL

Put ice in a small tumbler and pour over vodka, Cointreau and lime cordial. Stir well.

INTIMATE

2 ICE CUBES
20 ML/¾ FL OZ VODKA
20 ML/¾ FL OZ APRICOT BRANDY
20 ML/¾ FL OZ DRY VERMOUTH
2 DASHES ORANGE BITTERS
1 BLACK OLIVE
PIECE OF LEMON PEEL

Put ice in a mixing glass with vodka, apricot brandy, vermouth and bitters. Stir and strain into a cocktail glass. Decorate with olive and lemon peel, and serve with a cocktail stick.

LIGHT BLUE

ICE CUBES
25 ML/1 FL OZ VODKA
15 ML/½ FL OZ BLUE CURAÇAO
15 ML/½ FL OZ LEMON JUICE
1 DASH ORGEAT SYRUP
1 COCKTAIL CHERRY
1 LEMON SLICE

Crack ice and put into shaker with vodka, curaçao, lemon juice and orgeat syrup. Shake well and strain into a cocktail glass. Decorate with cherry and a slice of lemon on a cocktail stick.

MARGARITA

SALT
2–3 ICE CUBES
25 ML/1 FL OZ TEQUILA
15 ML/½ FL OZ COINTREAU
15 ML/½ FL OZ LIME or LEMON JUICE

Dip rim of a cocktail glass first in water, shaking off excess, then in salt. Allow frosting to dry. Crack ice and put in a shaker with other ingredients. Shake and strain into glass.

RED TONIC

25 ML/1 FL OZ VODKA
25 ML/1 FL OZ GRENADINE
10 ML/2 TEASPOONS LEMON JUICE
1 ICE CUBE
1 LEMON SLICE
TONIC WATER

Put vodka, grenadine and lemon juice in a mixing glass and stir well. Strain into a tall glass. Add ice and lemon slice and top up with tonic water. Serve with a straw.

MOSCOW MULE

ICE CUBES
25 ML/1 FL OZ VODKA
25 ML/1 FL OZ LIME CORDIAL
GINGER BEER
SQUEEZE OF FRESH LIME
1 SLICE OF LIME
1 SLICE OF LEMON

Put ice into a tall tumbler and pour over vodka and lime cordial. Top up with ginger beer, and add a squeeze of fresh lime. Decorate with slice of lime and lemon.

SCREWDRIVER

2–3 ICE CUBES
80 ML/3 FL OZ ORANGE JUICE
25 ML/1 FL OZ VODKA
1 ORANGE SLICE

Put ice in a mixing glass with orange juice and vodka. Stir very well and strain into a tumbler. Fix orange slice on rim of glass and serve with a straw.

SPUTNIK (1) AND (2)

SPUTNIK (1)

4–6 ICE CUBES
65 ML/2½ FL OZ VODKA
25 ML/1 FL OZ FERNET BRANCA
5 ML/1 TEASPOON LEMON JUICE
2.5 ML/½ TEASPOON CASTER SUGAR

Crack half ice and put in a shaker with other
ingredients. Shake well and strain into a large
cocktail glass. Add remaining ice.

SPUTNIK (2)

2–3 ICE CUBES
25 ML/1 FL OZ VODKA
15 ML/½ FL OZ BRANDY
15 ML/½ FL OZ BOURBON WHISKY
SANGRITA
CAYENNE PEPPER

Crack ice and put in a shaker with vodka, brandy
and whisky. Shake well and strain into a
tumbler. Top up with sangrita. Sprinkle with
Cayenne pepper, and stir well.

Tequila Caliente

2–3 ICE CUBES
40 ML/1½ FL OZ TEQUILA
15 ML/½ FL OZ CRÈME DE CASSIS
15 ML/½ FL OZ LIME JUICE
2 DASHES GRENADINE
SODA WATER

Put ice in a small tumbler with tequila, crème de cassis, lime juice and grenadine. Stir well and add a shot of soda water. Serve with a straw.

Tequila Fix

15 ML/½ FL OZ LIME JUICE
10 ML/2 TEASPOONS HONEY
50 ML/2 FL OZ TEQUILA
2 DASHES COINTREAU
4–5 ICE CUBES
1 LEMON SLICE

Put lime juice and honey in a tall tumbler and stir well. Add tequila and Cointreau. Crush ice and add to glass. Stir well and decorate with lemon slice. Serve with a straw.

Tequila Cocktail

2–3 ICE CUBES
25 ML/1 FL OZ TEQUILA
20 ML/¾ FL OZ PORT
5 ML/1 TEASPOON LIME JUICE
2 DASHES ANGOSTURA BITTERS

Crack ice and put in a shaker with other ingredients. Shake and strain into a cocktail glass.

Tequila Cocktail

TEQUILA SUNRISE

6–8 ICE CUBES
50 ML/2 FL OZ TEQUILA
25 ML/1 FL OZ GRENADINE
25 ML/1 FL OZ LEMON JUICE
SODA WATER
1 LIME SLICE

Crack half ice and put in a shaker with tequila,
grenadine and lemon juice. Shake and strain
into a tumbler. Top up with soda water, add
remaining ice and fix lime slice on rim of glass.
Serve with a straw.

VODKA CRUSTA

15 ML/½ FL OZ ORANGE JUICE
15 ML/1 TABLESPOON CASTER SUGAR
4–5 ICE CUBES
40 ML/1½ FL OZ VODKA
15 ML/½ FL OZ BRANDY
15 ML/½ FL OZ RED VERMOUTH
1 DASH ORANGE BITTERS
1 DASH ANGOSTURA BITTERS
SPIRAL OF LEMON PEEL

Dip rim of a goblet first in orange juice, shaking
off excess, then in sugar. Allow frosting to dry.
Crack ice and put in a shaker with vodka,
brandy, vermouth, bitters and two teaspoons of
remaining sugar. Shake well and strain into
goblet. Decorate with spiral of lemon peel.

TOVARICH

8 ICE CUBES
50 ML/2 FL OZ VODKA
25 ML/1 FL OZ KÜMMEL
20 ML/¾ FL OZ LIME JUICE

Crack two ice cubes and put in a shaker with
vodka, kümmel and lime juice. Shake well.
Crush remaining ice and put in a tall, narrow
goblet. Strain in contents of shaker and serve
with a straw.

VODKA DAISY

4–6 PINEAPPLE CHUNKS
4–6 ICE CUBES
50 ML/2 FL OZ VODKA
10 ML/2 TEASPOONS SUGAR SYRUP
5 ML/1 TEASPOON BÉNÉDICTINE
1 DASH MARASCHINO
1 DASH CALVADOS
SODA WATER

Put pineapple chunks in a tall champagne glass.
Crack ice and put in a shaker with vodka, sugar
syrup, Bénédictine, maraschino and Calvados.
Shake very well and strain into glass. Add a shot
of soda water and serve with a straw and a spoon.

Vodka Fizz

3 ICE CUBES
50 ML/2 FL OZ PINEAPPLE JUICE
40 ML/1½ FL OZ VODKA
5 ML/1 TEASPOON LEMON JUICE
5 ML/1 TEASPOON SUGAR SYRUP
SODA WATER

Crack two ice cubes and put in a shaker with pineapple juice, vodka, lemon juice and sugar syrup. Shake very well and strain into a tall goblet. Top up with soda water, add remaining ice cube and serve with a straw.

Vodkatini

ICE CUBES
50 ML/2 FL OZ VODKA
10 ML/2 TEASPOONS DRY VERMOUTH
PIECE OF LEMON PEEL

Put ice in a mixing glass with vodka and vermouth, and stir well. Strain into a cocktail glass and squeeze lemon peel over the top. Decorate with lemon peel.

Vodka Gibson

2–3 ICE CUBES
40 ML/1½ FL OZ VODKA
15 ML/½ FL OZ DRY VERMOUTH
2–3 PEARL ONIONS

Put ice in a mixing glass with vodka and vermouth. Stir well and strain into a cocktail glass. Decorate with pearl onions and serve with a cocktail stick.

White Russian

2–3 ICE CUBES
40 ML/1½ FL OZ VODKA
15 ML/½ FL OZ COFFEE LIQUEUR
A SHOT OF SINGLE CREAM

Put ice in a shaker with other ingredients and shake well. Pour into a tumbler.

BROOKLYN

WHISKY-BASED COCKTAILS

BROOKLYN

2–3 ICE CUBES
25 ML/1 FL OZ WHISKY
25 ML/1 FL OZ DRY VERMOUTH
10 ML/2 TEASPOONS MARASCHINO
3 DASHES AMER PICON
1 COCKTAIL CHERRY

Crack ice and put in a shaker with whisky, vermouth, maraschino and Amer Picon. Shake well and strain into a cocktail glass. Decorate with cherry.

Bourbon Cocktail

2–3 ICE CUBES
25 ML/1 FL OZ BOURBON WHISKY
10 ML/2 TEASPOONS BÉNÉDICTINE
10 ML/2 TEASPOONS COINTREAU
10 ML/2 TEASPOONS LEMON JUICE
1 DASH ANGOSTURA BITTERS

Crack ice and put in a shaker with other ingredients. Shake well and strain into a cocktail glass.

Cape Kennedy

2–3 ICE CUBES
20 ML/¾ FL OZ ORANGE JUICE
20 ML/¾ FL OZ LEMON JUICE
5 ML/1 TEASPOON WHISKY
5 ML/1 TEASPOON RUM
5 ML/1 TEASPOON BÉNÉDICTINE
5 ML/1 TEASPOON SUGAR SYRUP

Crack ice and put in a shaker with other ingredients. Shake well and strain into a cocktail glass.

CAPE KENNEDY

65

Bourbon Highball

4 ICE CUBES
25 ML/1 FL OZ BOURBON WHISKY
SODA WATER or GINGER ALE
SPIRAL OF LEMON PEEL

Put ice and whisky in a tumbler. Add soda water or ginger ale to taste. Decorate with spiral of lemon peel, and serve with a straw.

Irish Coffee

10 ML/2 TEASPOONS CASTER SUGAR
40 ML/1½ FL OZ IRISH WHISKY
STRONG HOT COFFEE
15 ML/½ FL OZ CREAM

Put sugar in a goblet and add whisky. Top up with coffee, and stir. Add cream, pouring it gently over back of a spoon so that it floats on surface.

Cowboy

4 ICE CUBES
40 ML/1½ FL OZ WHISKY
25 ML/1 FL OZ CREAM

Crush ice and put in a shaker with whisky and cream. Shake and strain into a small goblet. Serve with a straw.

Knockout

2–3 ICE CUBES
1 EGG YOLK
10 ML/2 TEASPOONS SUGAR SYRUP
25 ML/1 FL OZ SCOTCH WHISKY
SPARKLING WINE

Crack ice and put in a shaker. Add egg yolk, sugar syrup and whisky. Shake well and strain into a tall glass. Top up with sparkling wine and serve with a straw.

LIEUTENANT

2–3 ICE CUBES
25 ML/1 FL OZ BOURBON WHISKY
15 ML/½ FL OZ APRICOT BRANDY
15 ML/½ FL OZ GRAPEFRUIT JUICE
5 ML/1 TEASPOON SUGAR SYRUP
1 COCKTAIL CHERRY

Crack ice and put in a shaker with whisky, apricot brandy, grapefruit juice and sugar syrup. Shake and strain into a cocktail glass. Decorate with cherry and serve with a cocktail stick.

MANHATTAN SWEET

2–3 ICE CUBES
25 ML/1 FL OZ BOURBON WHISKY
25 ML/1 FL OZ BIANCO VERMOUTH
1 DASH ANGOSTURA BITTERS

Put ice in a mixing glass with whisky, vermouth and bitters. Stir well and strain into a goblet.

MANHATTAN DRY

2–3 ICE CUBES
40 ML/1½ FL OZ BOURBON WHISKY
15 ML/½ FL OZ DRY VERMOUTH
1 DASH ANGOSTURA BITTERS

Put ice in a mixing glass with whisky, vermouth and bitters. Stir well and strain into a goblet.

MONTE CARLO COCKTAIL

2–3 ICE CUBES
40 ML/1½ FL OZ CANADIAN WHISKY
15 ML/½ FL OZ BÉNÉDICTINE
2 DASHES ANGOSTURA BITTERS

Crack ice and put in a shaker with other ingredients. Shake and strain into a cocktail glass.

MARY QUEEN OF SCOTS

15 ML/½ FL OZ LEMON JUICE
15 ML/1 TABLESPOON CASTER SUGAR
2–3 ICE CUBES
25 ML/1 FL OZ SCOTCH WHISKY
15 ML/½ FL OZ DRAMBUIE
15 ML/½ FL OZ GREEN CHARTREUSE
1 COCKTAIL CHERRY

Dip rim of a cocktail glass first in lemon juice, shaking off excess, then in sugar. Allow frosting to dry. Crack ice and put in a shaker with whisky, Drambuie and Chartreuse. Shake and strain into glass. Spear cherry on a cocktail stick and use to decorate.

MORNING GLORY FIZZ

2–3 ICE CUBES
1 EGG WHITE
10 ML/2 TEASPOONS CASTER SUGAR
25 ML/1 FL OZ LEMON JUICE
50 ML/2 FL OZ BOURBON WHISKY
5 ML/1 TEASPOON PERNOD
SODA WATER

Crush ice and put in a shaker with egg white, sugar, lemon juice, whisky and Pernod. Shake very well and strain into a tumbler or balloon glass. Top up with soda water and serve with a straw.

MARY QUEEN OF SCOTS

NEW YORKER

2–3 ICE CUBES
40 ML/1½ FL OZ BOURBON WHISKY
15 ML/½ FL OZ LEMON JUICE
5 ML/1 TEASPOON GRENADINE
PIECE OF ORANGE PEEL

Crack ice and put in a shaker with whisky, lemon juice and grenadine. Shake and strain into a cocktail glass. Squeeze orange peel over top.

MISSISSIPPI

2–3 ICE CUBES
25 ML/1 FL OZ RYE WHISKY
25 ML/1 FL OZ RUM
25 ML/1 FL OZ LEMON JUICE
2 DASHES SUGAR SYRUP
SPIRAL OF LEMON PEEL

Crack ice and put in a shaker with whisky, rum,
lemon juice and sugar syrup. Shake and strain
into a small goblet. To decorate, wind lemon
peel round a wooden skewer or spear it on a
cocktail stick.

OLD-FASHIONED

5 ML/1 TEASPOON CASTER SUGAR
5 ML/1 TEASPOON WATER
2 DASHES ANGOSTURA BITTERS
2–3 ICE CUBES
50 ML/2 FL OZ BOURBON WHISKY
1 ORANGE SLICE
1 COCKTAIL CHERRY

Put sugar, water and bitters in a small tumbler
and stir well. Add ice and whisky. Stir again.
Decorate with orange slice and cherry.

MISSISSIPPI

OLD PAL

2–3 ICE CUBES
25 ML/1 FL OZ BOURBON WHISKY
15 ML/½ FL OZ DRY VERMOUTH
15 ML/½ FL OZ CAMPARI
PIECE OF LEMON PEEL

Put ice in a mixing glass with whisky, vermouth
and Campari. Stir well and strain into a cocktail
glass. Add lemon peel.

69

Rabbit's Revenge

2–3 ICE CUBES
40 ML/1½ FL OZ BOURBON WHISKY
25 ML/1 FL OZ PINEAPPLE JUICE
2–3 DASHES GRENADINE
TONIC WATER
1 ORANGE SLICE

Put ice in a shaker with whisky, pineapple juice and grenadine. Shake well and pour into a tumbler. Top up with tonic water and fix orange slice on rim of glass. Serve with a straw.

Rob Roy

2–3 ICE CUBES
25 ML/1 FL OZ SCOTCH WHISKY
25 ML/1 FL OZ RED VERMOUTH
1 DASH ANGOSTURA BITTERS
1 COCKTAIL CHERRY

Put ice in a mixing glass with whisky, vermouth and bitters. Stir well and strain into a cocktail glass. Decorate with cherry and serve with a cocktail stick.

Red Shadow

2–3 ICE CUBES
25 ML/1 FL OZ WHISKY
15 ML/½ FL OZ APRICOT BRANDY
15 ML/½ FL OZ CHERRY BRANDY
5 ML/1 TEASPOON LEMON JUICE

Crack ice and put in a shaker with other ingredients. Shake well and strain into a cocktail glass.

Rusty Nail

2–3 ICE CUBES
40 ML/1½ FL OZ SCOTCH WHISKY
20 ML/¾ FL OZ DRAMBUIE
SPIRAL OF LEMON PEEL

Put ice in a small tumbler. Add whisky and Drambuie, and stir. Decorate with lemon peel.

Rye Cocktail

2–3 ICE CUBES
50 ML/2 FL OZ RYE WHISKY
2–3 DASHES GRENADINE
2 DASHES ANGOSTURA BITTERS
1 COCKTAIL CHERRY

Put ice in a mixing glass with whisky, grenadine and bitters. Stir well and strain into a small goblet. Spear cherry on a cocktail stick and use to decorate.

Sheep's Head

3 ICE CUBES
40 ML/1½ FL OZ BOURBON WHISKY
15 ML/½ FL OZ RED VERMOUTH
5 ML/1 TEASPOON BÉNÉDICTINE
PIECE OF LEMON PEEL
1 COCKTAIL CHERRY

Put ice in a mixing glass with whisky, vermouth and Bénédictine. Stir and strain into a small tumbler. Squeeze lemon peel over top and decorate with cherry. Serve with a straw.

Rye Daisy

3–4 ICE CUBES
40 ML/1½ FL OZ RYE WHISKY
20 ML/¾ FL OZ YELLOW CHARTREUSE
10 ML/2 TEASPOONS LEMON JUICE
5 ML/1 TEASPOON SUGAR SYRUP
SODA WATER
2 PEACH SLICES
2 STRAWBERRIES

Crack ice and put in a shaker with whisky, Chartreuse, lemon juice and sugar syrup. Shake well and strain into a small goblet. Top up with soda water and decorate with peach slices and strawberries. Serve with a straw and a spoon.

Stone Fence

2–3 ICE CUBES
50 ML/2 FL OZ WHISKY
CIDER
SPIRAL OF APPLE PEEL

Put ice in a medium-sized tumbler and add whisky. Top up with cider and decorate with spiral of apple peel.

Wine-based and Non-alcoholic Cocktails

Adonis

Adonis

3 ICE CUBES
25 ML/1 FL OZ SHERRY
20 ML/¾ FL OZ RED VERMOUTH
1 DASH ANGOSTURA BITTERS

Put ice in a mixing glass with other ingredients.
Stir and strain into a cocktail glass.

AMERICAN COOLER

3 ICE CUBES
100 ML/4 FL OZ RED WINE
25 ML/1 FL OZ RUM
15 ML/½ FL OZ SUGAR SYRUP
5 ML/1 TEASPOON ORANGE JUICE
5 ML/1 TEASPOON LEMON JUICE
SODA WATER
1 LEMON SLICE

Put ice in a tall tumbler with wine, rum, sugar syrup, orange juice and lemon juice. Stir well and top up with soda water. Fix lemon slice on rim of glass.

BAMBOO

2 ICE CUBES
25 ML/1 FL OZ DRY VERMOUTH
25 ML/1 FL OZ SHERRY
2 DASHES ANGOSTURA BITTERS
1 DASH ORANGE BITTERS
1 COCKTAIL CHERRY
PIECE OF LEMON PEEL

Put ice, vermouth, sherry, Angostura and orange bitters in a mixing glass. Stir well. Strain into a cocktail glass and decorate with cherry. Squeeze lemon peel over top and serve with a straw.

AMERICANO

3 ICE CUBES
25 ML/1 FL OZ RED VERMOUTH
25 ML/1 FL OZ CAMPARI
SODA WATER
PIECE OF LEMON RIND

Put ice in a tumbler with vermouth and Campari. Stir and top up with soda water. Decorate with piece of lemon rind and serve with a straw.

BAMBOO

73

AMOUR CRUSTA

15 ML/½ FL OZ LEMON JUICE
15 ML/1 TABLESPOON CASTER SUGAR
2–3 ICE CUBES
50 ML/2 FL OZ TAWNY PORT
5 ML/1 TEASPOON COINTREAU
5 ML/1 TEASPOON MARASCHINO
2 DASHES PEACH BITTERS
2 DASHES LIME JUICE
SPIRAL OF LEMON PEEL

Dip rim of a cocktail glass first in lemon juice, shaking off excess, then in sugar. Allow frosting to dry. Crack ice and put in a shaker with remaining ingredients except lemon peel. Shake well and strain into glass. Decorate with lemon peel.

BUTLER'S GOOD MORNING FLIP

2 ICE CUBES
1 EGG
1 EGG YOLK
10 ML/2 TEASPOONS CASTER SUGAR
40 ML/1½ FL OZ SHERRY
3 DASHES ANGOSTURA BITTERS
SPARKLING WINE

Crush ice and put in a shaker with egg, egg yolk, sugar, sherry and bitters. Shake very well and pour into a large cocktail glass. Top up with sparkling wine and serve with a straw.

BUCK'S FIZZ

80 ML/3 FL OZ ORANGE JUICE
CHAMPAGNE

Put orange juice in a tall tumbler and top up with champagne.

CAMPARI AND SODA

2–3 ICE CUBES
40 ML/1½ FL OZ CAMPARI
SODA WATER
SPIRAL OF LEMON PEEL

Put ice in a large tumbler, add Campari and top up with soda water to taste. Decorate with spiral of lemon peel, and serve with a straw.

CAMPINO

15 ML/½ FL OZ CAMPARI
15 ML/½ FL OZ DRY VERMOUTH
15 ML/½ FL OZ RED VERMOUTH
15 ML/½ FL OZ GIN
2 DASHES CRÈME DE CASSIS
SODA WATER
SPIRAL OF ORANGE PEEL

Put Campari, vermouths, gin and crème de cassis in a mixing glass. Top up with soda water, and stir. Pour into a small tumbler and decorate with spiral of orange peel.

CHAMPAGNE DAISY

2–3 ICE CUBES
20 ML/¾ FL OZ YELLOW CHARTREUSE
20 ML/¾ FL OZ LEMON JUICE
10 ML/2 TEASPOONS GRENADINE
CHAMPAGNE
FRUIT IN SEASON

Crack ice and put in a shaker with Chartreuse, lemon juice and grenadine. Shake well and strain into a shallow champagne glass. Top up with champagne and decorate with pieces of fruit. Serve with a cocktail stick and a straw.

CHAMPAGNE COCKTAIL

1 SUGAR LUMP
2 DASHES ANGOSTURA BITTERS
1 ICE CUBE
15 ML/½ FL OZ BRANDY
CHAMPAGNE
PIECE OF LEMON PEEL

Put sugar lump in a champagne glass and soak with bitters. Add ice and brandy, and top up with champagne. Squeeze lemon peel over top. Serve with a straw.

CHOCOLATE COCKTAIL

2–3 ICE CUBES
40 ML/1½ FL OZ PORT
10 ML/2 TEASPOONS CRÈME DE CACAO
10 ML/2 TEASPOONS YELLOW CHARTREUSE
5 ML/1 TEASPOON GRATED BITTER CHOCOLATE

Crack ice and put in a shaker with other ingredients. Shake well and strain into a cocktail glass.

CRYSTAL HIGHBALL

JEUNE HOMME

2–3 ICE CUBES
25 ML/1 FL OZ DRY VERMOUTH
15 ML/½ FL OZ GIN
15 ML/½ FL OZ COINTREAU
15 ML/½ FL OZ BÉNÉDICTINE
1 DASH ANGOSTURA BITTERS

Crack ice and put in a shaker with other
ingredients. Shake and strain into a large
cocktail glass.

CRYSTAL HIGHBALL

1–2 ICE CUBES
20 ML/¾ FL OZ BIANCO VERMOUTH
20 ML/¾ FL OZ RED VERMOUTH
20 ML/¾ FL OZ ORANGE JUICE
SODA WATER
SPIRAL OF ORANGE PEEL

Put ice in a large cocktail glass. Add vermouths
and orange juice, and stir. Top up with soda
water and decorate with spiral of orange peel.
Serve with a straw.

KIR

15 ML/½ FL OZ CRÈME DE CASSIS
DRY WHITE WINE

Put crème de cassis in wine glass and top up with
wine.

MANHATTAN COOLER

4 ICE CUBES
80 ML/3 FL OZ CLARET
15 ML/½ FL OZ LEMON JUICE
3 DASHES RUM
10 ML/2 TEASPOONS CASTER SUGAR
GINGER ALE
1 COCKTAIL CHERRY

Crack two ice cubes and put in a shaker with claret, lemon juice, rum and sugar. Shake very well and strain into a tall goblet. Top up to taste with ginger ale. Add cherry and remaining ice.

MYRA

2–3 ICE CUBES
25 ML/1 FL OZ RED WINE
15 ML/½ FL OZ VODKA
15 ML/½ FL OZ VERMOUTH

Put ice in a mixing glass with other ingredients. Stir well and strain into a cocktail glass.

MOONLIGHT

3–4 ICE CUBES
40 ML/1½ FL OZ BIANCO VERMOUTH
15 ML/½ FL OZ PEAR BRANDY

Put ice in a mixing glass with vermouth and pear brandy. Stir well and strain into a cocktail glass.

MOONLIGHT

PIMM'S

2–3 ICE CUBES
40 ML/1½ FL OZ PIMM'S NO 1
2 ORANGE SLICES
1 LEMON SLICE
LEMONADE
SPIRAL OF CUCUMBER PEEL or SPRIG OF MINT

Put ice in a tall tumbler. Add Pimm's and orange and lemon slices. Top up with lemonade and decorate with spiral of cucumber peel or sprig of mint.

SHERRY COBBLER

4 ICE CUBES
2 ORANGE SLICES
1 LEMON SLICE
65 ML/2½ FL OZ SHERRY
15 ML/½ FL OZ SUGAR SYRUP

Crush ice and put in a tall tumbler or tall champagne glass. Halve orange and lemon slices and add to glass. Pour in sherry and sugar syrup. Stir, and serve with a straw.

RAY LONG

3 ICE CUBES
25 ML/1 FL OZ BIANCO VERMOUTH
20 ML/¾ FL OZ BRANDY
5 ML/1 TEASPOON PERNOD
1 DASH ANGOSTURA BITTERS

Put ice in a mixing glass with other ingredients. Stir well and strain into a cocktail glass.

VERMOUTH CASSIS

2–3 ICE CUBES
80 ML/3 FL OZ DRY VERMOUTH
40 ML/1½ FL OZ CRÈME DE CASSIS
SODA WATER
PIECE OF LEMON PEEL

Put ice in a goblet with vermouth and crème de cassis. Stir and top up with soda water. Decorate with piece of lemon peel and serve with a straw.

Grapefruit Highball

2–3 ICE CUBES
80 ML/3 FL OZ GRAPEFRUIT JUICE
25 ML/1 FL OZ GRENADINE
SODA WATER or GINGER ALE

Put ice in a tall tumbler with grapefruit juice and grenadine. Top up with soda water or ginger ale, stir, and serve with a straw. This highball may also be served in a hollowed-out grapefruit half.

Prairie Oyster

5 ML/1 TEASPOON WORCESTERSHIRE SAUCE
1 EGG YOLK
10 ML/2 TEASPOONS TOMATO KETCHUP
2 DASHES LEMON JUICE
2 DASHES OLIVE OIL
SALT, PEPPER, PAPRIKA

Put Worcestershire sauce in a shallow glass. Slide in egg yolk. Add tomato ketchup, lemon juice, olive oil, salt, pepper and paprika. Do not stir this drink, but swallow it in one gulp.

Orange Cooler

3–4 ICE CUBES
10 ML/2 TEASPOONS CASTER SUGAR
100 ML/4 FL OZ ORANGE JUICE
GINGER ALE

Put ice in a large tumbler with sugar and orange juice. Stir and top up with ginger ale. Serve with a straw.

Tomato Cocktail

2–3 ICE CUBES
50 ML/2 FL OZ TOMATO JUICE
2 DASHES LEMON JUICE
1 DASH TOMATO KETCHUP
1 DASH WORCESTERSHIRE SAUCE
CELERY SALT

Crack ice and put in a shaker with tomato juice, lemon juice, tomato ketchup, Worcestershire sauce and a little celery salt. Shake well and strain into a small goblet.

Index